D1195344

STATE PROFILES

FLORIDA

BY COLLEEN SEXTON

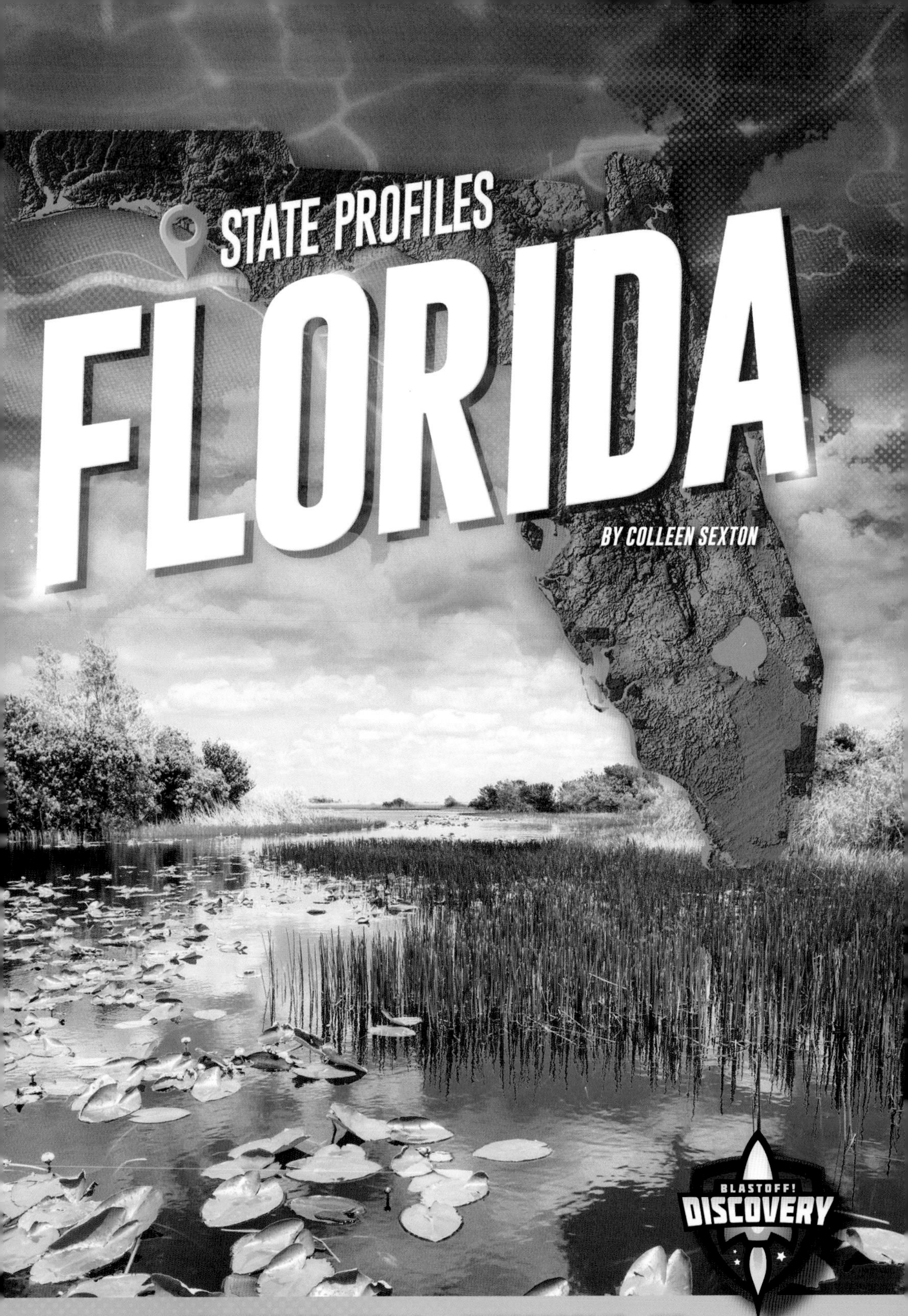

BELLWETHER MEDIA • MINNEAPOLIS, MN

Blastoff! Discovery launches a new mission: reading to learn. Filled with facts and features, each book offers you an exciting new world to explore!

BLASTOFF! UNIVERSE

BLASTOFF! Beginners — GRADE K

BLASTOFF! READERS — GRADES 1-3

BLASTOFF! DISCOVERY — GRADE 4

This edition first published in 2022 by Bellwether Media, Inc.

No part of this publication may be reproduced in whole or in part without written permission of the publisher.
For information regarding permission, write to Bellwether Media, Inc.,
Attention: Permissions Department,
6012 Blue Circle Drive, Minnetonka, MN 55343.

Library of Congress Cataloging-in-Publication Data

Names: Sexton, Colleen A., 1967- author.
Title: Florida / by Colleen Sexton.
Description: Minneapolis, MN : Bellwether Media, Inc., 2022. |
  Series: Blastoff! Discovery: State profiles | Includes bibliographical
  references and index. | Audience: Ages 7-13 | Audience: Grades
  4-6 | Summary: "Engaging images accompany information about
  Florida. The combination of high-interest subject matter and narrative
  text is intended for students in grades 3 through 8"– Provided by
  publisher.
Identifiers: LCCN 2021019677 (print) | LCCN 2021019678 (ebook)
  | ISBN 9781644873816 (library binding) | ISBN
  9781648341588 (ebook)
Subjects: LCSH: Florida–Juvenile literature.
Classification: LCC F311.3 .S47 2022 (print) | LCC F311.3 (ebook)
  | DDC 975.9–dc23
LC record available at https://lccn.loc.gov/2021019677
LC ebook record available at https://lccn.loc.gov/2021019678

Editor: Rebecca Sabelko   Designer: Kathleen Petelinsek

Printed in the United States of America, North Mankato, MN.

TABLE OF CONTENTS

NINE MILE POND
EVERGLADES

It is a sunny winter's day in Florida's Everglades National Park. A family begins a kayaking adventure on Nine Mile Pond. The family follows a trail through shallow marsh waters. They wind around sawgrasses and **mangrove islands**. At times, the mangrove trees form tunnels.

HOW BIG IS IT?

Everglades National Park covers more than 2,410 square miles (6,242 square kilometers) of wetlands in southern Florida.

OTHER TOP SITES

BUSCH GARDENS TAMPA BAY

KENNEDY SPACE CENTER

SAINT AUGUSTINE LIGHTHOUSE AND MARITIME MUSEUM

WALT DISNEY WORLD RESORT

Later, the family trades kayaks for bicycles. They pedal through Shark Valley. Along the way, they see herons, egrets, and other marsh birds. Alligators crawl near the trail. The family stops to climb a 65-foot (19.8-meter) observation tower. The Everglades spread as far as they can see. Welcome to Florida!

ALABAMA

Florida is a southeastern state that covers 65,758 square miles (170,312 square kilometers). Most of Florida is a **peninsula**. It includes a string of islands called the Florida Keys. The southernmost island is Key West.

The Atlantic Ocean crashes upon Florida's eastern shore. The **Straits** of Florida wash upon the southern coast. The **Gulf** of Mexico lies to the west. Alabama wraps around Florida's panhandle in the northwest. Georgia shares the rest of the state's northern border. The capital, Tallahassee, sits in the panhandle. Other major cities include Jacksonville, Miami, and Tampa.

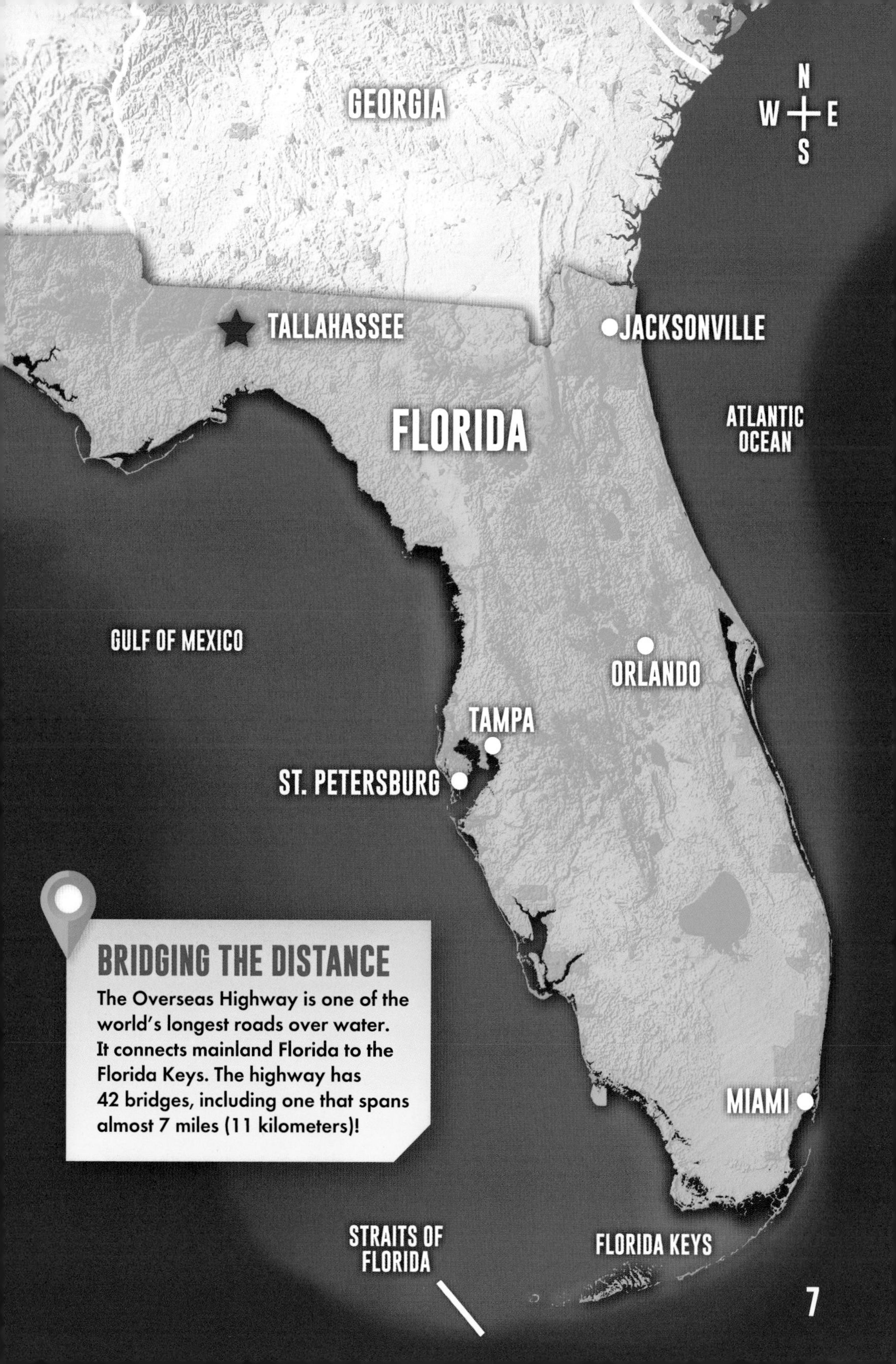

GEORGIA

N
W E
S

★ TALLAHASSEE

●JACKSONVILLE

FLORIDA

ATLANTIC
OCEAN

GULF OF MEXICO

●ORLANDO

●TAMPA

ST. PETERSBURG ●

BRIDGING THE DISTANCE

The Overseas Highway is one of the world's longest roads over water. It connects mainland Florida to the Florida Keys. The highway has 42 bridges, including one that spans almost 7 miles (11 kilometers)!

MIAMI ●

STRAITS OF
FLORIDA

FLORIDA KEYS

TIMUCUA VILLAGE

The first people arrived in Florida about 12,000 years ago. Their **descendants** included the Apalachee, Calusa, and Timucua tribes. In 1513, explorer Juan Ponce de León landed on Florida's Atlantic coast. He claimed the land for Spain.

JUAN PONCE DE LEÓN

Soon, **settlers** from Spain and other parts of Europe arrived. They brought diseases, and many Native Americans died. The United States took control of Florida in 1821. The government forced some Native Americans to move west when farmers wanted more land. In 1845, Florida became a state. It fought for the South during the **Civil War** from 1861 to 1865.

NATIVE PEOPLES OF FLORIDA

SEMINOLE TRIBE OF FLORIDA

- Original lands in Florida, Georgia, Alabama, and parts of South Carolina, Tennessee, and Mississippi
- More than 4,000 members today

MICCOSUKEE TRIBE OF INDIANS OF FLORIDA

- Originally part of the Creek Nation from Georgia and Alabama
- More than 600 in Florida today

Low hills and forests cover the Florida Uplands in northern and central Florida. Many lakes dot this region. Coastal **plains** make up the rest of the state. The Everglades, Big Cypress Swamp, and other wetlands spread across southern Florida. Rich farmland produces crops in the southwest. The shorelines feature long sandy beaches. **Barrier islands** line Florida's coasts. **Coral reefs** lie just offshore.

N
W + E
S

■ FLORIDA UPLANDS
■ EVERGLADES
□ BIG CYPRESS SWAMP

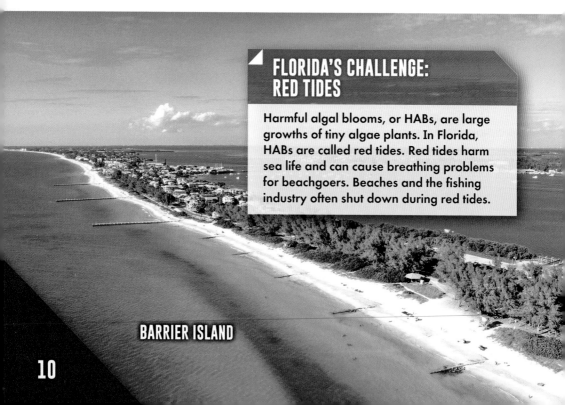

FLORIDA'S CHALLENGE: RED TIDES

Harmful algal blooms, or HABs, are large growths of tiny algae plants. In Florida, HABs are called red tides. Red tides harm sea life and can cause breathing problems for beachgoers. Beaches and the fishing industry often shut down during red tides.

BARRIER ISLAND

SPRING
HIGH: 81°F (27°C)
LOW: 61°F (16°C)

SUMMER
HIGH: 90°F (32°C)
LOW: 73°F (23°C)

FALL
HIGH: 83°F (28°C)
LOW: 65°F (18°C)

WINTER
HIGH: 70°F (21°C)
LOW: 51°F (11°C)

°F = degrees Fahrenheit
°C = degrees Celsius

BIG CYPRUS SWAMP

Florida is sunny, warm, and **humid** much of the year. Ocean breezes help cool the coasts during hot summers. **Hurricanes** can bring strong winds and heavy rains to the coasts.

11

Florida is full of wildlife. Alligators live throughout the state. They glide through swamps, rivers, and lakes. These waters are also home to bass, bluegills, and other freshwater fish. Eagles, ospreys, and other birds of prey grab fish in their talons. Crocodiles dig nests in the far southern tip of Florida. Manatees, dolphins, and whales swim in coastal waters.

The rare Florida panther prowls through wooded swamps. Opossums and wild pigs root around for fruit, insects, and small animals. Key deer are the smallest deer in North America. The only place they live is the Florida Keys.

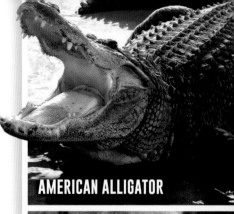

AMERICAN ALLIGATOR

FLORIDA PANTHER

FLAMINGO

KEY DEER

BLUSHING BIRDS

Florida is famous for pink flamingos. Their coloring comes from the algae and small shellfish that they eat.

FLORIDA MANATEE

Life Span: up to 60 years
Status: endangered

Florida manatee range = ■

| LEAST CONCERN | NEAR THREATENED | VULNERABLE | ENDANGERED | CRITICALLY ENDANGERED | EXTINCT IN THE WILD | EXTINCT |

More than 21 million people live in Florida. Cities are home to 9 out of every 10 Floridians. Most cities are on the state's coasts. The southeastern stretch between West Palm Beach and Miami is heavily populated.

WEST PALM BEACH

FLOCKING TO FLORIDA

Many older people from cold, northern states have moved to Florida. These retirees are known as snowbirds.

MIAMI BEACH

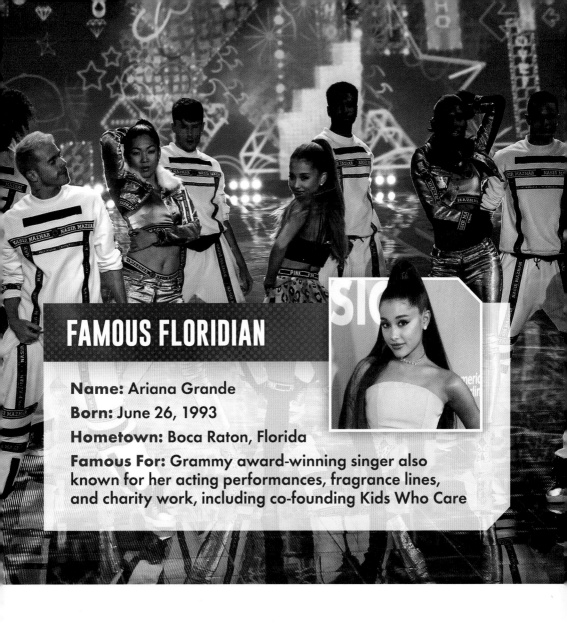

FAMOUS FLORIDIAN

Name: Ariana Grande
Born: June 26, 1993
Hometown: Boca Raton, Florida
Famous For: Grammy award-winning singer also known for her acting performances, fragrance lines, and charity work, including co-founding Kids Who Care

Many Floridians are descendants of Europeans. About one of every four residents is Hispanic. The largest Hispanic population is Cuban. Other Floridians have roots in Mexico, Puerto Rico, the Dominican Republic, Colombia, and Nicaragua. African Americans and Black people make up nearly one in five Floridians. Small numbers of Seminoles and Miccosukees live in the state.

THE MAGIC CITY

Miami is known as the Magic City. It grew so much during the 1890s that people said it appeared like magic.

SOUTH BEACH

Miami began as a village of Tequesta Indians many centuries ago. In 1896, it became a railroad stop. The city grew very quickly. Today, Miami is the state's second-largest city. It sits in southeastern Florida on Biscayne Bay at the mouth of the Miami River. The city is a **tourist** hot spot. Hotels rise along its sandy beaches.

Visitors and residents enjoy Cuban music, art, and food in Little Havana. Animal lovers explore Jungle Island and Zoo Miami. Bayside Marketplace draws locals to waterfront stores and restaurants. Every year, the city hosts cheering crowds for the Orange Bowl college football game.

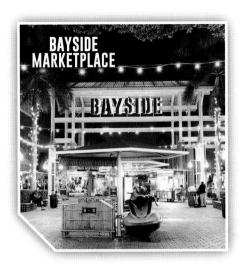

BAYSIDE MARKETPLACE

FLORIDA'S FUTURE: RISING SEAS

Climate change is causing sea levels to rise. In the future, the homes and businesses in Miami and other coastal areas will be underwater. Local governments must plan for Floridians in coastal areas to move to higher ground.

LITTLE HAVANA

In the early 1800s, citrus fruit production became a major industry in Florida. Today, the state is the country's leading grower of oranges and grapefruit. Processing these fruits into juice and other products is one of Florida's largest industries. Farmers also grow sugarcane and tomatoes. Beef cattle graze on pastures in central Florida.

Nearly 9 of every 10 Floridians have **service jobs**. Many work in hotels, theme parks, and resorts. Service workers also hold jobs in health care, banking, and real estate. Other Floridians work in fishing. Crews haul in crabs, lobsters, and shrimp from coastal waters. Factory workers **manufacture** computers and other electronic devices.

INVENTED IN FLORIDA

GATORADE

Date Invented: 1965

Inventors: Robert Cade, Dana Shires, H. James Free, and Alejandro de Quesada, University of Florida

FROZEN ORANGE JUICE CONCENTRATE

Date Invented: 1970s

Inventors: Cedric Donald Atkins, Edwin Moore, and Louis G. MacDowell

CUBAN SANDWICH

Florida's food reflects its **diversity** and **natural resources**. Cuban sandwiches feature roast pork, ham, Swiss cheese, mustard, and pickles. These ingredients are pressed between slices of toasted Cuban bread. Fish dishes are also popular. Cooks flavor grouper and snapper with fresh citrus. Some stews and chowders include alligator. Fried gator bites are also popular.

"Floribbean" dishes combine flavors brought by **immigrants** from around the world. Jerk chicken is a Floribbean favorite. Another is conch fritters. Cooks batter and fry meat from conch shellfish. Key lime pie is a sweet end to any meal. It features the juice of tiny limes grown in the Florida Keys.

JERK CHICKEN

KEY LIME PIE

8 SERVINGS

Have an adult help you make this sweet treat!

INGREDIENTS

1 unbaked graham cracker pie shell

1 14-ounce can sweetened condensed milk

3 egg yolks, beaten

1/2 cup key lime juice or lime juice

DIRECTIONS

1. Preheat the oven to 375 degrees Fahrenheit (191 degrees Celsius).

2. Combine the egg yolks, sweetened condensed milk, and lime juice. Mix well.

3. Pour the mix into the pie shell.

4. Bake for 15 minutes. Let cool.

5. Top with whipped cream and lime slices.

DAYTONA 500

Floridians are big sports fans. Crowds cheer for professional football, basketball, hockey, and baseball teams. Many major league baseball teams head to the state for spring training every year. *Jai alai* is a popular sport similar to handball. NASCAR racing fans enjoy the Daytona 500 at Daytona Beach.

SPRING TRAINING

On Florida's beaches, surfers ride the waves and snorkelers explore coral reefs. Floridians enjoy swimming, boating, and fishing on both coastal and inland waters. The Everglades attracts bird-watchers. Kennedy Space Center at Cape Canaveral offers popular guided tours. In Orlando, Walt Disney World provides family fun.

DESTINATION DISNEY

Walt Disney World is the most popular theme park in the world. More than 50 million people visit every year!

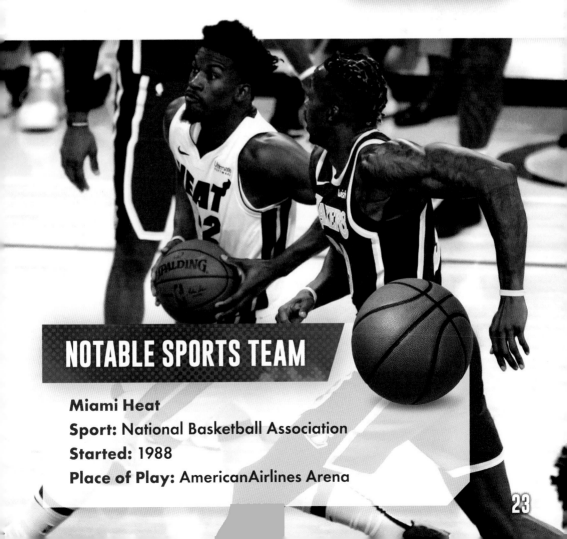

NOTABLE SPORTS TEAM

Miami Heat
Sport: National Basketball Association
Started: 1988
Place of Play: AmericanAirlines Arena

GASPARILLA PIRATE FEST

Every January, the Gasparilla Pirate Fest kicks off with a pirate crew sailing into Tampa. The pirates take over the city and hand out treasure during a grand parade! The celebration continues with a street festival. Plant City hosts the Strawberry Festival in March. This huge food festival features carnival rides, livestock shows, and big-name musical performances.

The Calle Ocho Music Festival in March covers 20 blocks in Miami's Little Havana. It is the country's largest Hispanic festival. Musical acts perform on several stages. Crowds dance the *salsa* and *merengue* to Latin beats. Florida's festivals showcase the state's diverse communities!

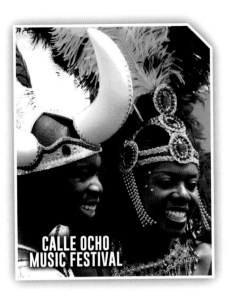

CALLE OCHO MUSIC FESTIVAL

STRAWBERRY FESTIVAL

1513
Spanish explorer Juan Ponce de León lands in Florida and claims it for Spain

1868
Florida rejoins the United States

1845
Florida becomes the 27th state

1565
Saint Augustine is established as the first permanent European settlement in America

1861
Florida leaves the United States to fight with the Confederacy in the Civil War

2010

The Deepwater Horizon oil spill harms wildlife in the Gulf of Mexico

1960s

Many Cubans move to Florida because they are unhappy with their government

1947

Everglades National Park is established

2021

The Tampa Bay Buccaneers win the Super Bowl

1971

Walt Disney World opens in Orlando

Nicknames: The Sunshine State, The Everglades State, The Orange State, The Peninsula State

State Motto: In God We Trust

Date of Statehood: March 3, 1845 (the 27th state)

Capital City: Tallahassee ★

Other Major Cities: Jacksonville, Miami, Tampa, Orlando, St. Petersburg

Area: 65,758 square miles (170,312 square kilometers); Florida is the 22nd largest state.

Population
21,538,187
(2020)

STATE FLAG

Adopted in 1900, Florida's state flag has red diagonal bars on a white background. The state seal is in the center of the flag. It features a palm tree, a steamship on water, and a Seminole woman scattering flowers. Sun rays are in the background. The state's name and motto circle the seal.

INDUSTRY

Main Exports

MANUFACTURING
3%

FARMING AND NATURAL RESOURCES
1%

GOVERNMENT
10%

SERVICES
86%

JOBS

aircraft parts

cell phones

computer parts

perfumes

Natural Resources

water, petroleum, phosphate, limestone, clay, sand, gravel

GOVERNMENT

Federal Government
28 | 2
REPRESENTATIVES | SENATORS

30
ELECTORAL VOTES

USA

FL

State Government
120 | 40
REPRESENTATIVES | SENATORS

STATE SYMBOLS

STATE BIRD
NORTHERN MOCKINGBIRD

STATE SALTWATER FISH
ATLANTIC SAILFISH

STATE FLOWER
ORANGE BLOSSOM

STATE TREE
SABAL PALM TREE

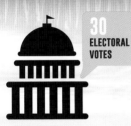

GLOSSARY

barrier islands—long, sandy islands along a shore created by wind and waves

Civil War—a war between the Northern (Union) and Southern (Confederate) states that lasted from 1861 to 1865

coral reefs—structures made of coral that usually grow in shallow seawater

descendants—people related to a person or group of people who lived at an earlier time

diversity—having a variety of people or things from many different backgrounds

gulf—part of an ocean or sea that extends into land

humid—having a lot of moisture in the air

hurricanes—storms formed in the tropics that have violent winds and often have rain and lightning

immigrants—people who move to a new country

mangrove islands—groups of trees that grow in tropical climates in salty swamp water

manufacture—to make products, often with machines

natural resources—materials in the earth that are taken out and used to make products or fuel

peninsula—a section of land that extends out from a larger piece of land and is almost completely surrounded by water

plains—large areas of flat land

service jobs—jobs that perform tasks for people or businesses

settlers—people who move to live in a new, undeveloped region

straits—narrow channels connecting two large bodies of water

tourist—a person who travels to visit another place

AT THE LIBRARY

Holub, Joan. *Where Is Walt Disney World?* New York, N.Y.: Penguin Workshop, 2018.

Nelson, Penelope S. *Everglades National Park.* Minneapolis, Minn.: Jump!, 2020.

Orr, Tamra B. *Florida.* New York, N.Y.: Children's Press, 2018.

ON THE WEB

FACTSURFER

Factsurfer.com gives you a safe, fun way to find more information.

1. Go to www.factsurfer.com.

2. Enter "Florida" into the search box and click ○.

3. Select your book cover to see a list of related content.

INDEX